THE LINCOLN MEMORIAL

★ ★

THE
LINCOLN MEMORIAL

DILLON PRESS
New York

Maxwell Macmillan Canada
Toronto
Maxwell Macmillan International
New York   Oxford   Singapore   Sydney

by Catherine Reef

Photo Credits

Front cover: John Blank
Back cover: John Reef
Frontispiece: John Blank
AP—Wide World Photos: 8, 57, 60, 67; The Bettmann Archive: 13, 23, 39, 48, 54; John Reef: 15, 40, 64, 68; The Granger Collection: 16, 31, 37; Surratt House Museum: 28, 35

Library of Congress Cataloging-in-Publication Data

Reef, Catherine.
    The Lincoln Memorial / by Catherine Reef. — 1st ed.
        p. cm. — (Places in American history)
    Includes index.
    Summary: Provides a detailed history of the planning and construction of the national monument honoring Abraham Lincoln.
    ISBN 0-87518-624-6
    1. Lincoln Memorial (Washington, D.C.)—Juvenile literature. 2. Washington (D.C.)—Buildings, structures, etc.—Juvenile literature. 3. Lincoln, Abraham, 1809-1865—Monuments—Washington (D.C.) —Juvenile literature. [1. Lincoln Memorial (Washington, D.C.) 2. National monuments.] I. Title. II. Series.
F203.4.L73R38 1994
975.3—dc20   93-13708

Dillon Press   Maxwell Macmillan Canada, Inc.
Macmillan Publishing Company   1200 Eglinton Ave. East
866 Third Ave.   Suite 200
New York, NY   10022   Don Mills, Ontario   M3C 3N1

Macmillan Publishing Company is part of the Maxwell Communication Group of Companies.

First Edition

Printed in the United States of America

10 9 8 7 6 5 4 3 2 1

CONTENTS

Points of Interest

1. U.S. Capitol
2. White House
3. Lincoln Memorial
4. Vietnam Veterans Memorial
5. Washington Monument
6. Jefferson Memorial
7. Smithsonian Institution
8. John F. Kennedy Center for the Performing Arts
9. Ford's Theatre
10. Supreme Court
11. Library of Congress
12. Pentagon Building

PLACES IN AMERICAN HISTORY

Lincoln Memorial

GEORGIA AVE.

MASSACHUSETTS AVE.

PENNSYLVANIA AVE.

CONSTITUTION AVE.

The Mall

INDEPENDENCE AVE.

CAPIT HIL

Tidal Basin

Potomac River

Washington D.C.

Washington, D.C.

N

VIRGINIA

I-395

Anacostia River

0   1¼ Miles

0   1¼ Kilometers

CHAPTER 1

ENSHRINED FOREVER

Long before the sun came up on August 28, 1963, buses and trains were already arriving in Washington, D.C. They carried people from all over the United States. The people had come to the nation's capital to demand jobs and equal treatment for African Americans.

By 7:30 A.M., a crowd had gathered at the base of the Washington Monument, the tall marble shaft that honors George Washington. The crowd grew as the morning passed. Both black and white people came. Some of the men wore business suits; others wore denim overalls, outfits they called "freedom uniforms." Young women stood beside grandmothers. Many clergymen joined the gathering.

The air grew hot and humid, and the sky turned the hazy gray of a Washington summer day. Shortly after 11:00 A.M., the crowd began to march. Constitution and Independence avenues, two wide, tree-lined thoroughfares, became rivers of moving people. Marchers filled the grassy space between the avenues, an area known as the Mall. Many in the crowd carried signs that told the world why they were marching. WE DEMAND EQUAL RIGHTS! read some of the signs. WE MARCH FOR INTEGRATED SCHOOLS NOW! GOD OF JUSTICE, GOD OF POWER, CAN AMERICA DENY FREEDOM IN THIS HOUR?

As the mass of people moved forward, an old man and his wife fell behind. The gray-haired couple took their time, and at last they finished the .8-mile march. "All the groups passed us," the old man told a reporter, "but we just kept on walking."

Over the many heads in the crowd, the couple saw the Lincoln Memorial. They looked

A view of the Lincoln Memorial taken from a helicopter on August 28, 1963

upon a marble structure with columns and tall steps. Inside, they knew, was a statue of Abraham Lincoln, the 16th president of the United States. The statue depicted a seated and weary president, looking out on the city from which he had led his nation.

The monument to Lincoln was a fitting destination for a freedom march. Lincoln is remembered as a man who loved liberty and democracy. He was the president who ended slavery in the United States and guided the nation to victory in the Civil War. In this bloody conflict, which lasted from 1861 until 1865, U.S. forces defeated the armies of 11 Southern states. The Southern states had broken away from the Union to form their own nation, the Confederacy. Lincoln's wise leadership during this crisis proved to the world that America's democratic government would endure.

The Lincoln Memorial is located at the west end of the Mall, close to other structures of historic importance. To the north is the White House, home of the president. The U.S. Capitol, the building in which Congress makes the nation's laws, is two miles to the east. From the memorial's steps, visitors can look across the long, shallow Reflecting Pool to the Washington Monument. The memorial to Thomas Jefferson, the nation's third president, sits among cherry trees to the south.

The Lincoln Memorial stands beside the Potomac River, with Arlington National Cemetery on the opposite bank. Established during the Civil War, this military cemetery is the burial place of heroes from every American war, from the American Revolution through the Persian Gulf War.

The Lincoln Memorial's closest neighbor is also its newest. The Vietnam Veterans Memorial, nearly hidden by trees and walkways, honors the Americans who died in the military conflict in Vietnam during the 1960s and 1970s.

American forces had not yet entered the war in Vietnam on August 28, 1963, when the crowd of 200,000 listened to speeches given from the steps of the Lincoln Memorial. As the speakers voiced their thoughts about equality and freedom, they carried on the tradition of Abraham Lincoln. Lincoln is known as a great speaker and writer. In speeches such as the Gettysburg Address and Second Inaugural Address, Lincoln expressed the goals of democracy in words that people have treasured.

The Reverend Martin Luther King, Jr., was the last person to speak on the occasion of the March on Washington. Standing before the crowd at the Lincoln Memorial, King gave another inspiring speech that set forth democratic ideals. King, a Baptist minister from the South, had become a leader in the growing civil rights movement. He had led African Americans in other peaceful demonstrations against racism. More than once, his protests had landed him in jail.

Martin Luther King, Jr., delivers his "I Have a Dream" speech.

"I have a dream," King told the nation on that August day. "It is a dream deeply rooted in the American dream. I have a dream that one day this nation will rise up and live out the meaning of its creed, 'We hold these truths to be self-evident, that all men are created equal.'"

King encouraged his audience "to work together, to pray together, to struggle together, to go to jail together, to stand up for freedom together."

With King's words echoing in their hearts, the listeners returned to their buses and trains. They traveled home, knowing they had helped to make history. They had been part of the largest political demonstration the nation had ever seen. The March on Washington would be remembered as a peaceful event, a time when many thousands of Americans came together to express a common goal.

Thirty years after the marchers gathered in Washington, the Lincoln Memorial remains a monument to freedom. Every year, more than one million people climb its five flights of stairs to view the 19-foot-high statue of Abraham Lincoln. They read the words of the Gettysburg Address and the Second Inaugural Address, which are carved into the monument's walls. They study the murals on those walls, which

FOUR SCORE AND SEVEN YEARS
AGO OUR FATHERS BROUGHT FORTH
ON THIS CONTINENT A NEW NATION
CONCEIVED IN LIBERTY AND DEDICA-
TED TO THE PROPOSITION THAT ALL
MEN ARE CREATED EQUAL·
NOW WE ARE ENGAGED IN A GREAT
CIVIL WAR TESTING WHETHER THAT
NATION OR ANY NATION SO CON-
CEIVED AND SO DEDICATED CAN LONG
ENDURE· WE ARE MET ON A GREAT
BATTLEFIELD OF THAT WAR· WE HAVE
COME TO DEDICATE A PORTION OF
THAT FIELD AS A FINAL RESTING
PLACE FOR THOSE WHO HERE GAVE
THEIR LIVES THAT THAT NATION
MIGHT LIVE· IT IS ALTOGETHER FIT-
TING AND PROPER THAT WE SHOULD
DO THIS· BUT IN A LARGER SENSE
WE CAN NOT DEDICATE· WE CAN NOT
CONSECRATE· WE CAN NOT HALLOW-
THIS GROUND· THE BRAVE MEN LIV-
ING AND DEAD WHO STRUGGLED HERE
HAVE CONSECRATED IT FAR ABOVE
OUR POOR POWER TO ADD OR DETRACT·
THE WORLD WILL LITTLE NOTE NOR
LONG REMEMBER WHAT WE SAY HERE
BUT IT CAN NEVER FORGET WHAT THEY
DID HERE· IT IS FOR US THE LIVING
RATHER TO BE DEDICATED HERE TO
THE UNFINISHED WORK WHICH THEY
WHO FOUGHT HERE HAVE THUS FAR
SO NOBLY ADVANCED· IT IS RATHER FOR
US TO BE HERE DEDICATED TO THE
GREAT TASK REMAINING BEFORE US-
THAT FROM THESE HONORED DEAD
WE TAKE INCREASED DEVOTION TO
THAT CAUSE FOR WHICH THEY GAVE THE
LAST FULL MEASURE OF DEVOTION-
THAT WE HERE HIGHLY RESOLVE THAT
THESE DEAD SHALL NOT HAVE DIED IN
VAIN-THAT THIS NATION UNDER GOD
SHALL HAVE A NEW BIRTH OF FREEDOM-
AND THAT GOVERNMENT OF THE PEOPLE
BY THE PEOPLE FOR THE PEOPLE SHALL
NOT PERISH FROM THE EARTH·

Lincoln's Gettysburg Address, inscribed at the Lincoln Memorial

depict Lincoln's democratic beliefs.

At the Lincoln Memorial, visitors honor Abraham Lincoln's ideas and his contributions. Lincoln preserved the United States in the Civil War and worked to end slavery not just for the Americans of his own time, but for every generation that has followed. The words inscribed above Lincoln's statue are as meaningful today as when they were carved, more than 70 years ago: "In this temple, as in the hearts of the people for whom he saved the Union, the memory of Abraham Lincoln is enshrined forever."

CHAPTER 2

FATHER ABRAHAM

Thousands of people had gathered outside the U.S. Capitol on the crisp morning of March 4, 1861. They had come to see Abraham Lincoln sworn in as the 16th president of the United States. Soldiers mingled with the crowd. They lined the city streets, watching for signs of a disturbance. It was a troubled time, a time when emotions might cause people to act violently. The United States, still a young nation, seemed to be splitting apart.

The issue of slavery had divided the American people. The South had grown into a great agricultural region where crops of cotton, tobacco, and sugar brought in profits. But those profits were earned at the expense of four million

Lincoln arrives at the Capitol for his 1861 inauguration.

people—the African-American slaves who toiled in the fields and served in their masters' homes. White Americans in the South claimed it was their right to own black slaves. Many other Americans, living primarily in the North, insisted that slavery was wrong.

During the 1800s, Americans were moving west into new states and territories. Settlers from the South wanted to bring their slaves along. Throughout the North, people reacted with anger. Some of these people, called abolitionists, favored outlawing slavery everywhere. Many more were willing to let slavery continue in the South. They objected, though, to the idea that slavery might spread.

The members of Congress tried to please people on both sides of the slavery issue. One of their agreements, the Missouri Compromise of 1820, allowed Missouri to join the Union as a slave state. At the same time, Maine became a new state in which slavery was outlawed.

The Missouri Compromise divided the west into two sections: a southern section where slavery would be legal, and a northern section where it would not.

Thirty-four years later, a new law permitted the people of Kansas and Nebraska to decide for themselves whether they wanted slavery. The Kansas-Nebraska Act caused an uproar. According to the Missouri Compromise, Kansas and Nebraska were to be forever free from slavery.

One person who spoke out against slavery was a lawyer from Illinois. In 1858, Abraham Lincoln ran for election to the U.S. Senate. Lincoln insisted that slavery violated the ideas expressed in the Declaration of Independence. "We began by declaring that all men are created equal," Lincoln said, "but now from that beginning we have run down to the other declaration, that for some men to enslave others is 'a sacred right of self-government.'" Lincoln believed that the time had come for the question of slavery to be settled. "This government cannot endure, permanently half slave and half free," he stated.

Lincoln lost the election to the Senate, but in 1860, the Republican party chose him to run for president of the United States. Southerners feared that if Lincoln won the election, he would work to end slavery everywhere. The citizens of South Carolina threatened to secede, or withdraw, from the United States if Lincoln became president.

Abraham Lincoln was elected president in November 1860, and South Carolina seceded in December. By March 4, 1861, when Lincoln walked to the speaker's platform in front of the U.S. Capitol, seven Southern states had seceded from the Union. They had formed a new nation, the Confederate States of America. Four more states seemed ready to follow.

The tall, bearded man put on his steel-rimmed glasses. He looked out at the crowd and spoke in a high-pitched voice. In this speech, his

First Inaugural Address, Lincoln asked the Southern states to return to the nation peacefully. "We are not enemies, but friends," he told the Southern people. He reminded them that soldiers from the North and South had fought together for American independence. Strong bonds linked the North and South, Lincoln said. He called those bonds "mystic chords of memory, stretching from every battlefield and patriot grave, to every living heart and hearthstone, all over this broad land."

Lincoln pledged that he would not end slavery in the states where it already existed. But his words failed to persuade the people of the South. On April 12, Confederate cannons opened fire on Fort Sumter, a U.S. military installation that stood on an island outside Charleston, South Carolina. The attack on Fort Sumter marked the start of the American Civil War.

Abraham Lincoln had grown up in the Kentucky wilderness, far from towns or cities. He had completed less than one year of school. Now, from his office in the White House, this self-educated pioneer faced the greatest crisis in the history of the nation. President Lincoln ordered Union ships to blockade Southern ports. He called out the militia, private citizens who had been trained as soldiers. He asked for 75,000 more men to join the armed forces. Across the North, patriotic citizens hurried to volunteer. They believed the war would be a quick one. The Union might win it with only one battle.

Their first battle taught the Union troops that beating the Confederates would be harder than they had thought. On July 21, 1861, the Union army attacked the Southern forces at Manassas , Virginia, 25 miles from Washington, D.C. The U.S. troops charged bravely across a creek known as Bull Run. They battled with rifles, bayonets, and cannons. But after a few hours of fighting, the poorly trained Union soldiers retreated in panic. They left behind

The Battle of Bull Run

hundreds of dead and wounded men. President Lincoln watched from a White House window as the muddy, bleeding survivors stumbled into the capital.

One Union loss followed another in the months ahead. In the spring of 1862, General George McClellan led the army south in an attempt to capture Richmond, Virginia, the Confederate capital. Weeks of marching and fighting under McClellan's command resulted in 23,000 soldiers killed, wounded, or missing—and no victories.

In August, General John Pope led a second attack at Bull Run. The army suffered another defeat, losing 25,000 men. "You need to command the commanders!" Attorney General Edward Bates told Lincoln. The president spent many nights reading military books so that he could plan battles and advise his generals.

The first months of the war were a troubled time for the Lincoln family as well. The president's wife, Mary, had relatives in the South. A few were even fighting for the Confederacy. Some people said that Mrs. Lincoln herself was disloyal to the United States. These false claims upset her greatly.

Then, in February 1862, one of the Lincolns' sons, 11-year-old Willie, died from an illness. "My poor boy," Lincoln said. "He was too good for this earth." Mary Lincoln was too shaken by her son's death to attend the funeral. For three months, she refused to leave her bedroom. "Try and control your grief," counseled her worried husband, "or it will drive you mad." Mary worked hard to conquer her sorrow, but she never fully recovered from Willie's death.

As Lincoln's family struggled with its loss and the nation struggled in battle, the president turned to the problem of slavery. The abolitionists were urging him to free the slaves. "Teach the rebels and traitors that the price they are to pay for the attempt to abolish the Government must be the abolition of slavery," counseled Frederick Douglass, a writer, speaker, and former slave.

Lincoln's advisers told him that ending slavery would help the war effort. Thousands of slaves had been put to work to aid the Southern cause. Once free, they might willingly fight for the Union. "You need more men," Senator Charles Sumner said to Lincoln. "You need the slaves."

From the beginning of the war, Lincoln's goal had been to unite his divided country, even if that meant allowing slavery in the South. He feared that many soldiers—men who would die for their country—might refuse to fight for the slaves. Also, slavery still existed in four Union states: Maryland, Delaware, Kentucky, and Missouri. If Lincoln outlawed slavery, these "border states" might secede and join the Confederacy.

On September 17, 1862, the Union won a battle near Antietam Creek in Maryland. It was a day of heavy losses, a day when the bodies of soldiers covered the battlefield. Still, the Union troops had caused the Southern army to retreat. Lincoln saw this victory as a sign that God wanted the slaves to be emancipated, or freed.

Five days later, Lincoln read his Emancipation Proclamation to his closest advisers. This historic document stated that, beginning January 1, 1863, any slaves living in Confederate-held territory would be free, "thenceforward and forever." Lincoln signed the proclamation on New Year's Day. "If my name ever goes into history," he said, "it will be for this act."

With the Emancipation Proclamation, the Civil War became a fight to unite the nation— and to free the slaves. The army opened its ranks to African Americans. By the war's end, more than 180,000 black men would fight for the Union. They would take part in more than 400 battles across the South.

In the summer of 1863, the Confederate

Lincoln and his cabinet look over the Emancipation Proclamation.

army marched north into Pennsylvania. Union
forces met them in the small town of Gettysburg.
For three hot July days, the two armies fought
on the hills and farms of Gettysburg. The battle
left 51,000 men dead or wounded. The people of
Pennsylvania created a cemetery in Gettysburg for the slain Union soldiers. They invited

President Lincoln to speak at the dedication ceremony.

On November 19, 1863, Lincoln stood before a crowd of 15,000 people who had gathered at the new cemetery. The president had planned his remarks while traveling to Gettysburg by train. "It is what I would call a short, short speech," he had confided to a friend. The speech was so short that Lincoln delivered it in just two minutes. This disappointed many of the people present, who liked to hear long talks, full of flowery language. Yet Lincoln's Gettysburg Address is considered one of the greatest speeches in American history.

Lincoln spoke to his audience about their heritage as Americans. "Four score and seven years ago," he began, "our fathers brought forth upon this continent, a new nation, conceived in Liberty, and dedicated to the proposition that all men are created equal." Lincoln said that the purpose of the Civil War was to test "whether that nation, or any nation so conceived, and so dedicated, can long endure." The soldiers buried at Gettysburg had died in the struggle to preserve their nation. It was up to the living to continue that struggle, Lincoln concluded, so that "government of the people, by the people, for the people, shall not perish from the earth."

On March 4, 1865, Lincoln again faced a large audience. He had been reelected as president, and he had come to the U.S. Capitol to be sworn in once more. The years of war had taken a toll on the president whom many Americans now called "Father Abraham." A friend noted that Lincoln's face appeared "haggard with care, tempest tossed and weatherbeaten."

Now the war was nearly over. The Union forces had gained control of the Mississippi River, an important shipping route that flowed through the Confederacy. Union soldiers had captured the city of Atlanta, Georgia. They had marched across the state to Savannah,

Lincoln's Second Inauguration

destroying everything in their path.

Lincoln's speech on that March day was nearly as short as the Gettysburg Address. In a spirit of healing, he asked the American people to welcome the defeated Southerners back into the Union "with malice toward none; with charity for all; with firmness in the right as God gives us to see the right." He urged his fellow Americans "to do all which may achieve and cherish a just and lasting peace among ourselves, and with all nations."

CHAPTER 3

A SHRINE FOR ALL

General Robert E. Lee, commander of the Confederate army, surrendered at Appomattox Court House, Virginia, on April 9, 1865. The Civil War had ended, and the states of the North and South were once again a single nation. As the people of Washington, D.C., celebrated the victory with fireworks and music, President Lincoln started to heal his nation's wounds. He asked a band to play "Dixie," a favorite song of the Confederate soldiers. "I have always thought 'Dixie' one of the best tunes I ever heard," he said.

On April 14, five days after the surrender, Lincoln and his wife decided to go out for the evening. They attended a performance at Ford's

Theatre in Washington. As the Lincolns laughed out loud at the play, which was a popular comedy, a man approached the president from behind. Suddenly, the audience heard a gunshot, followed by Mary Lincoln's screams. A bullet had struck the president.

Who had committed this hateful crime? The audience soon found out. The well-known actor John Wilkes Booth leaped from the balcony where the president sat, shouting *"Sic semper tyrannis"*—a Latin phrase meaning "Thus always to tyrants."

Booth escaped as soldiers carried the stricken president to a house across the street. (Federal troops would later capture and kill Booth in a Virginia barn.) Lincoln had received a serious head wound, and the doctors who examined him offered no hope. "It is impossible for him to recover," said one.

Abraham Lincoln died on April 15, at 7:22 A.M., with friends and family present. "Now he belongs

The interior of Ford's Theatre on the night Lincoln was shot

to the ages," said Secretary of War Edwin
Stanton.

News of the president's death shocked the
nation. In Washington, thousands of mourners
lined up in the rain to file past his casket.
Lincoln's body then traveled by train to Spring-
field, Illinois, for burial. Everywhere the train
stopped, huge crowds came out to pay their
respects. Across the countryside, people lined up
along the railroad tracks and bowed their heads
as the black-draped train rumbled past.

Government officials and private citizens
talked about building a memorial to the beloved
president. They disagreed, though, about what it
should look like and where it should be. When
automobiles became popular in the early 20th
century, a congressman from Minnesota wanted
to build a highway between Washington, D.C.,
and Gettysburg, Pennsylvania, and name it
after Lincoln. Other people wanted to erect a
statue of Lincoln outside Washington's new

Lincoln's funeral procession in New York City

railroad station, or to place a memorial at
Arlington National Cemetery.

 To settle the matter, in 1911 Congress created
an organization called the Lincoln Memorial
Commission. The commission chose a site for
the memorial near the Potomac River, on a spot
where a swamp had recently been drained.
There, the memorial would sit between the U.S.
Capitol, an important symbol of the nation
Lincoln preserved, and Arlington National

Cemetery, the resting place of Union and Confederate soldiers. The commission also selected the architect Henry Bacon to design the memorial.

Bacon admired the temples of ancient Greece, elegant structures of white marble supported by rows of columns. He borrowed some ideas from the Greeks in his plan for the Lincoln Memorial. Bacon designed a structure 122 feet high, surrounded by 36 stone columns—one for each state that was in the Union at the time Lincoln died. Carved in the monument's exterior, above the columns, are the names of the 48 states that made up the nation when the memorial was built.

Laborers began to build the Lincoln Memorial in 1914. Because they were working on drained swampland, which offered little support, the workers built a foundation that was deep and strong. They anchored concrete pillars to the bedrock, far below the soft soil, to hold up the

The Lincoln Memorial under construction in 1918

heavy structure. They checked the foundation often while they were building the memorial. If it showed signs of settling, they repaired and strengthened it.

While the building took shape, Daniel Chester French started work on a statue of Lincoln to go inside. French was one of the best-known American sculptors of his time. Many people had praised his statues of George Washington, the Union general Ulysses S. Grant, and other historic figures.

As he planned his portrait in stone, French studied Lincoln's photographs and life masks—

impressions of the president's face that were molded while he was alive. French had been asked to create a statue 10 feet high, but he soon realized that a much bigger figure was needed to fill the space in the large memorial. French's finished statue stands 19 feet tall. Made from 22 blocks of white Georgia marble, the statue depicts Lincoln near the end of his life. The seated president appears wise and weary of war, patient and full of purpose.

There was much work to be done. Laborers paved roads and walkways leading to the memorial. Gardeners planted the area with bushes and trees. Work began on the Reflecting Pool, stretching between the Lincoln and Washington memorials. On sunny days, the water in this pool reflects both of these historic structures.

By 1922 the new Lincoln Memorial was finished. And on Memorial Day, May 30, 50,000 people gathered on the Mall to attend the dedication ceremony. As they listened to the speeches

Daniel Chester French's statue of Lincoln

given that day, thousands more listened with them on their radios at home. People across the United States marveled at this advance in technology. Radios had just begun to bring news and entertainment into people's homes.

The audience, both at the Mall and at home, heard William Howard Taft, Chief Justice of the Supreme Court, present the Lincoln Memorial to President Warren G. Harding. From 1909 until 1913, Taft himself had been president of the United States.

"The American people have waited fifty-seven years for a national monument to Abraham Lincoln," Taft said. He listed the personal qualities of Lincoln that the world admired. These included "justice, truth, patience, mercy, and love of his kind; simplicity, courage, sacrifice, and confidence in God."

Taft noted that the Lincoln Memorial, designed to resemble an ancient Greek temple, serves as a temple for modern Americans.

"Here is a shrine at which all can worship," he said. "Here is a sacred religious refuge in which those who love country and love God can find inspiration and repose."

The main speaker of the day was Robert Moton, president of the Tuskegee Institute in Alabama. Now called Tuskegee University, this school offered academic and professional courses to African Americans. "I speak for the Negro race," Moton told his fellow citizens. "Twelve million black Americans share in the rejoicing this day. As yet, no other name so warms the heart or stirs the depths of their gratitude as that of Abraham Lincoln."

Moton praised Lincoln's greatness. "Amid doubt and distrust," he said, "against the council of chosen advisers, in the hour of the Nation's utter peril, he put his trust in God and spoke the word that gave freedom to a race."

In his closing speech, Moton built upon the phrases of Lincoln's Second Inaugural Address:

"With malice toward none, with charity for all, with firmness in the right as God gives us to see the right, I somehow believe that all of us, black and white, both North and South, are going to strive on to finish the work which he so nobly began, to make America an example for the world of equal justice and equal opportunity."

CHAPTER 4

GATHERING FOR FREEDOM

Robert Moton spoke about racial equality. But when he finished his speech at the Lincoln Memorial, he sat down in a section of the audience reserved for African Americans. Like many places in the United States at that time, Washington, D.C., allowed segregation—the separation of blacks and whites.

Following the Civil War, Congress had passed three amendments, or revisions, to the Constitution. These amendments protected the rights of African Americans. The Thirteenth Amendment made slavery illegal in the United States. The Fourteenth Amendment granted citizenship to any person born in the United States. The Fifteenth Amendment granted black male citizens the right to vote. (Women gained the right to vote in 1920.)

These amendments, however, did not bring equality. New laws in southern states, laws known as "black codes," prevented African Americans from moving freely in society. These laws often spelled out the kinds of work black people could do, where they could gather, and when they could be on the streets. Other laws, so-called Jim Crow laws, separated blacks and whites in public. These laws called for separate schools for the two races, separate rest rooms and drinking fountains, separate waiting rooms in railroad stations, and more. Black and white passengers even had to sit separately on buses.

According to a Supreme Court ruling in 1896, this kind of segregation was legal. Local governments needed only to provide facilities for the two races that were "separate but equal," the Court said. A quick look, though, at the shabby schools and poor services for blacks was enough to convince anyone that the separate facilities were far from equal.

Although Jim Crow laws did not exist in the North, blacks faced inequality there as well. They often were restricted to low-paying jobs and houses in run-down neighborhoods because of their race.

Even fame did not protect African Americans from discrimination. In 1939, members of the black community in Washington, D.C., wished to invite Marian Anderson, an acclaimed African-American singer, to perform in their city. Anderson had earned a fine reputation singing throughout the United States and Europe. Washington's black citizens wanted Anderson to sing at Constitution Hall, the only large concert hall in the nation's capital at that time.

Constitution Hall is owned by the Daughters of the American Revolution (DAR), an organization of women whose ancestors fought in the

Marian Anderson sings on the front steps of the Lincoln Memorial

Revolutionary War. The DAR refused to let Marian Anderson appear on their stage. It was not to be used, they said, by a member of her race.

"I was saddened and ashamed," Anderson recalled. She was not angry at the DAR, but sorry for its members. "I felt that their behavior stemmed from a lack of understanding," she wrote. "They were doing something that was neither sensible nor good."

The First Lady at the time, Eleanor Roosevelt, was one member of the DAR who took a stand against the racist decision. She resigned from the organization in protest. "To remain as a member implies approval of that action," she stated.

The people of Washington still wanted to hear Marian Anderson sing, so some officials of the federal government offered her another concert site. They invited her to appear at the Lincoln Memorial.

On Easter Sunday, April 9, 1939, 75,000 people came together to hear Marian Anderson and support her right to perform. "There seemed to be people as far as the eye could see," the singer remembered. "The crowd stretched in a great semicircle from the Lincoln Memorial around the Reflecting Pool on to the shaft of the Washington Monument."

Anderson was so filled with emotion, she later admitted, that she feared she might be unable to sing. Yet she controlled her feelings and presented a program of patriotic songs, opera, arias, and spirituals. At the end of the recital, she thanked the many listeners for their applause and support. "I can't tell you what you have done for me today," she said.

Years later, the DAR changed its policy of segregation, allowing Marian Anderson and other black artists to appear at Constitution Hall. Anderson accepted an offer to perform there in a spirit of forgiveness. "It was a beautiful concert hall," she wrote, "and I was happy to sing in it."

The change at Constitution Hall was just one small gain in a larger struggle known as the civil rights movement. In 1954 the Supreme Court reversed its ruling on segregation—at least in public schools.

In 1955, a young minister from Birmingham, Alabama, Martin Luther King, Jr., led a boycott of the city's buses. Birmingham's black population refused to ride the buses until they received the same treatment as white customers. They achieved success when the Supreme Court outlawed segregation on buses.

Across the South, black Americans worked to gain other opportunities as well. They marched in the streets, demanding equal treatment. They staged sit-ins at restaurants that denied service to African Americans. They boycotted businesses that refused to hire blacks.

Some progress occurred slowly, but inequality remained. By 1963, the average white worker earned $6,500 a year, while the average black worker earned $3,500. Eleven percent of black workers were unemployed, while only 5 percent of whites lacked jobs. And many white southerners angrily resisted any effort by blacks to bring about change.

In June 1963, Alabama's governor, George Wallace, stood in a doorway at the University of Alabama so that two new black students could not enter. The students were able to attend their classes only when federal troops ordered Wallace to step aside.

The night of that incident, President John F. Kennedy spoke to the nation on television. The United States faced "a moral crisis as a nation and as a people," Kennedy said. "I am therefore asking Congress to enact legislation giving all Americans the right to be served in facilities which are open to the public—hotels, restaurants, theaters, retail stores and similar establishments."

One man who listened to the speech was 74-year-old A. Philip Randolph. As a young man, Randolph had founded the Brotherhood of Sleeping Car Porters, the first labor union to admit black railroad workers. Now, Randolph decided to organize a large demonstration in Washington, D.C. He hoped that many Americans would gather to show their support of Kennedy's civil rights law. Randolph wanted to draw attention to black workers' need for jobs.

That demonstration was the historic March on Washington. On August 28, 1963, Randolph spoke at the Lincoln Memorial. He faced the many thousands of people standing on the grass or cooling their tired feet in the Reflecting Pool. "Let the nation and the world know the meaning of our numbers," Randolph said. "We are the advance guard of a massive moral revolution for jobs and freedom."

Later in the day, Martin Luther King, Jr.,

Civil rights demonstrators line the path leading to the Lincoln Memorial in 1963.

addressed the crowd. His words touched the hearts of millions. The hopefulness and beauty of his words continue to inspire people today. "I have a dream that my four little children will one day live in a nation where they will not be judged by the color of their skin, but by the content of their character," King said.

King looked forward to the day, he said, "when all God's children, black men and white men, Jews and gentiles, Protestants and Catholics, will be able to join hands and sing in the words of the old Negro spiritual: 'Free at last. Free at last. Thank God almighty, we are free at last.'"

The new Civil Rights Act became law on July 2, 1964. Many people said that the March on Washington helped the law to pass. But the march did not end discrimination or racial hatred. Just 18 days after the gathering in Washington, an explosion killed four black children attending Bible school at a Birmingham, Alabama, church. In April 1968, a white assassin took the life of Martin Luther King, Jr.

In August 1983, 250,000 people came to the Lincoln Memorial to mark the 20th anniversary of the March on Washington. They came to honor the memory of Martin Luther King, Jr., and to affirm his goals. "Today is Martin's day," announced his widow, Coretta Scott King. "We are united by Martin's dream."

The crowd also voiced concern. Unemployment was still higher among African Americans than among whites, and salaries were still lower. "Twenty years later we have our freedom, our civil rights," said the Reverend Jesse Jackson, "but 20 years later we do not have equality."

Another crowd assembled at the Lincoln Memorial in August 1988, 25 years after the March on Washington. This time a large number of Hispanic Americans also marched for equality. Coretta Scott King welcomed their participation. As she explained, her husband's "dream of justice, equality and national unity is not the exclusive property of any race, religion or political party."

Many marchers brought their children to the

Twenty years after the 1963 march, African Americans returned to the Lincoln Memorial.

1988 event. The sight of so many young people showed the march's leaders that their struggle for peaceful change would continue. "The 1963 march was ancient history to them," said Julian Bond, a civil rights leader from Georgia, "but here they are."

To celebrate the 30th anniversary of the march on August 30, 1993, some 75,000 people returned to the steps of the Lincoln Memorial. Their presence there served to remind Americans of the work done by Martin Luther King, Jr.

CHAPTER 5

A MORNING AT THE MEMORIAL

The marble stairs of the Lincoln Memorial are worn from the pressure of many feet. They have supported the feet of presidents and ordinary citizens, of Marian Anderson and Martin Luther King, Jr.

The steps are slippery on this wet December morning. Parents reach for their children's hands. Aging men and women climb slowly and with care. A young couple bravely carry their infant daughter's stroller quickly to the top. The husband's pointed boots and cowboy hat show that this family has come from a western state.

After mounting the stairs, the visitors pass between the memorial's marble exterior columns, which are 44 feet in height. Measuring 7 feet

across at the base, the columns are as wide and as massive as the trunks of ancient trees. Some people turn to enjoy the view. It is a peaceful scene: the still waters of the Reflecting Pool, the spire of the Washington Monument, the familiar dome of the U.S. Capitol.

When the visitors step into the Lincoln Memorial's great central chamber, they have reached their goal. Here they stand on a floor of pink Tennessee marble. Far above their heads, beneath the 50-foot-high ceiling, two pigeons fly from one corner to another. Sunlight filters through panels of Alabama marble. The panels have been soaked in paraffin, a white, waxy substance, to make them translucent.

Soft, yellow light falls on the statue of Abraham Lincoln. Driving rain from a recent storm has coated the statue's knees and shoulders with dirt. But the simple dignity that sculptor Daniel Chester French labored to portray shows through clearly.

Fireworks light up the sky during a Fourth of July celebration, showing off the Washington Monument and the Lincoln Memorial.

People approach the figure of Lincoln quietly, with respect. Columns inside the memorial separate the central chamber from rooms to the north and south. A family from England stands between two of these columns and looks toward the north wall of the memorial, where Lincoln's Second Inaugural Address has been carved. They are silent as they read the famous words and study the mural above it.

The memorial's two murals, on the north and south walls, were painted by the American artist Jules Guérin. The images in these murals represent qualities for which Lincoln is admired and achievements for which he is honored. The mural on the north wall is titled *Reunion*. At its center, a golden-winged angel urges two robed figures to join hands. These figures symbolize the divided North and South coming together at the end of the Civil War. Figures to the right and left of this scene represent brotherhood and charity, feelings that Lincoln expressed as he welcomed the defeated South back into the Union.

Emancipation is the title of the south wall mural. In this painting, the angel is granting freedom to a slave. Seated figures in this mural stand for justice and eternity. Lincoln worked to free the African-American slaves because he was committed to justice, or fair treatment, for all people. He proclaimed that the slaves were to be forever free.

This mural hangs above the words of Lincoln's Gettysburg Address. Every day, people from places throughout the world read this famous speech from the Lincoln Memorial's south wall. No matter how many times they have heard its phrases, they are inspired by Lincoln's simple language and his heartfelt call for "a new birth of freedom."

The Lincoln Memorial is a place for taking pictures. All day long, visitors pose in front of the impressive statue of Lincoln. Parents and chil-

En route to the memorial, visitors pay their respects at the Vietnam Veterans Memorial.

dren, brothers and sisters, soldiers in uniform, clusters of friends—they all want photographs of themselves in this historic place. A group of tourists from Japan has arrived. They take turns standing before the statue, in twos and threes, while the others snap pictures.

Some visitors find their way down the stairs and into a gallery on the south side of the building. There, old photographs line the wall. The photographs are portraits of Abraham Lincoln taken at different times in his career. The first is the earliest known image of Lincoln, taken in 1846, when he was 38 years old. Lincoln sat for the last picture in 1865, shortly before his death. This final photograph shows a tired and aging president. "The young man had become an old man in less than twenty years," reads the caption below the photograph.

Two windows at the rear of this gallery give visitors a peek at the huge concrete pillars that support the Lincoln Memorial. When workers installed these windows in 1976, they found bottles and other objects that were left behind when the memorial was built. They saw that water seeping through the building's foundation had created stalactites and stalagmites. These deposits of minerals from the water hung like icicles and rose from the floor like pillars. An exhibit case holds some of the bottles, mineral formations, and other findings from 1976.

Rainwater, ice, and air pollution have begun to erode the Lincoln Memorial's walls. Birds have built nests in the structure, and countless insects have dashed themselves against it. In 1992 the National Park Service began a study of the Lincoln and Jefferson memorials. Researchers made detailed drawings of every marble block. They inspected the buildings inside and out, looking for signs of damage.

The inspection showed that the Lincoln Memorial's foundation needed repairs and waterproofing—work that requires the earth to be dug away from the foundation and concrete pillars, exposing them to the air. The dirt will be replaced when the work is complete, and new grass and trees will be planted. The researchers also observed that Guérin's murals have deteriorated greatly. Experts now face the challenge of restoring these paintings to their original appearance.

Work began on the Lincoln Memorial in

Each year National Park Service workers clean Lincoln's statue.

1914, and it goes on today. Americans continue
to honor the president who preserved their nation in a time of crisis. A grateful country main-
tains the Lincoln Memorial as a monument to
freedom and equality. Climbing the well-used
marble stairs, new generations mingle with old,

but all people from far and near come to the Lincoln Memorial to remember a great human being.

THE LINCOLN MEMORIAL: A HISTORICAL TIME LINE

1860 Abraham Lincoln is elected president of the United States. Southern states start to secede from the Union.

1861 Confederate forces attack Fort Sumter; the Civil War begins.

1863 Lincoln signs the Emancipation Proclamation, freeing the slaves in Confederate-held territory. The Union army defeats the Confederates at Gettysburg, Pennsylvania. Lincoln delivers the Gettysburg Address.

1865 Lincoln delivers his Second Inaugural Address. The Civil War ends in victory for the United States. Lincoln is assassinated at Ford's Theatre in Washington, D.C. The Thirteenth Amendment to the Constitution abolishes slavery.

1868 The Fourteenth Amendment makes former slaves citizens of the United States.

1870 The Fifteenth Amendment extends the right to vote to African-American males.

1911 Congress creates the Lincoln Memorial Commission.

1914 Construction of the Lincoln Memorial begins.

1922 The Lincoln Memorial is finished. The dedication ceremony takes place.

1939 Marian Anderson sings at the Lincoln Memorial.

1954 The Supreme Court outlaws segregation in public schools.

1955 Martin Luther King, Jr., leads a bus boycott in Montgomery, Alabama.

1956 The Supreme Court outlaws segregation on buses.

1963 The March on Washington takes place: 200,000 people gather at the Lincoln Memorial to demand jobs and equal treatment for African Americans. Martin Luther King gives his famous speech, "I Have a Dream."

1964 The Civil Rights Act becomes law.

1983 A crowd of 250,000 gathers at the Lincoln Memorial to mark the 20th anniversary of the March on Washington.

1988 Twenty-five years after the March on Washington, Americans come to the Lincoln Memorial to remember that historic event.

1992 The National Park Service begins a study of the Lincoln Memorial, to check for deterioration.

Visitor Information

Hours

The Lincoln Memorial is always open. A National Park Service ranger is present at the memorial from 8:00 A.M. until midnight, every day except Christmas.

Admission

Admission to the Lincoln Memorial is free.

Educational Programs

National Park Service rangers give informative talks about the Lincoln Memorial. The schedule for these talks is posted on a sign inside the memorial.

Special Events

On Lincoln's Birthday (February 12), an official of the United States government lays a wreath at the Lincoln Memorial. Speeches and music also mark the occasion.

For more information, contact:

The Lincoln Memorial
c/o The National Park Service
900 Ohio Drive, S.W.
Washington, DC 20242
(202) 426-6895

Index